A TRUE BOOK™

Planet Venus

CHRISTINE TAYLOR-BUTLER

Children's Press®
An Imprint of Scholastic Inc.
New York Toronto London Auckland Sydney
Mexico City New Delhi Hong Kong
Danbury, Connecticut

Content Consultant
Bryan C. Dunne
Assistant Chair, Assistant Professor Department of Astronomy
University of Illinois at Urbana–Champaign
Urbana, Illinois

Library of Congress Cataloging-in-Publication Data
Taylor-Butler, Christine.
 Planet Venus / by Christine Taylor-Butler.
   pages cm. — (A true book)
 Includes bibliographical references and index.
 ISBN 978-0-531-21159-5 (lib. bdg.) — ISBN 978-0-531-25365-6 (pbk.)
 1. Venus (Planet)—Juvenile literature. I. Title.
 QB621.T39 2014
 523.42—dc23   2013026505

All rights reserved. Published in 2014 by Children's Press, an imprint of Scholastic Inc.
Printed in China 62
SCHOLASTIC, CHILDREN'S PRESS, A TRUE BOOK™, and associated logos are trademarks and/or registered trademarks of Scholastic Inc.

4 5 6 7 8 9 10 R 23 22 21 20 19 18 17 16

**Front cover: Maat Mons,
a volcano on Venus**
**Back cover: The *Mariner 2*
spacecraft**

Find the Truth!

Everything you are about to read is true *except* for one of the sentences on this page.

Which one is **TRUE**?

T or F   The sun rises in the west on Venus.

T or F   The magnetic field on Venus is the same as on Earth.

Find the answers in this book.

3

Contents

THE BIG TRUTH!

Venus's surface is hot and covered by a thick, cloudy sky.

4 Visiting Earth's Neighbor

Twenty-five different spacecraft have visited Venus.

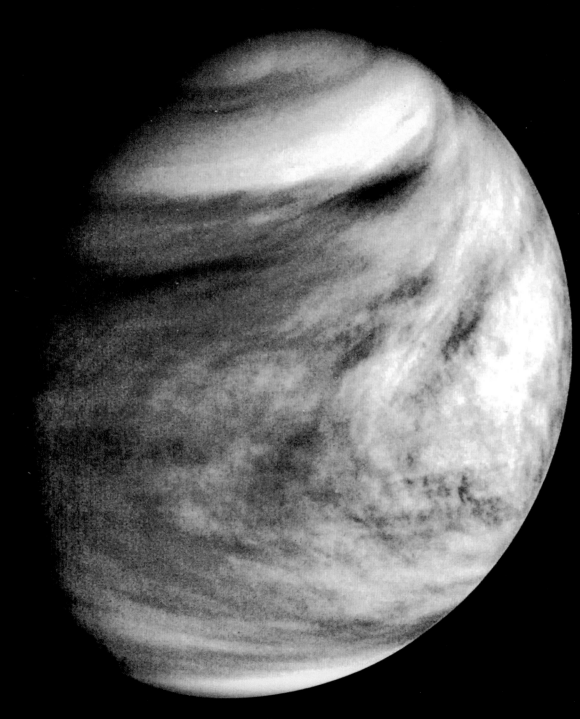

Earth's Twin?

Scientists once thought of the **planet** Venus as Earth's twin. Both have an **atmosphere**. They are similar in size and density. But Venus's swirling clouds hid its mysterious surface. People created theories about what the planet was like underneath the clouds. Some people even thought there was life on Venus. A French author believed Venusian civilization was advanced in art and music. But when people sent spacecraft to investigate, we learned Venus was not what it seemed.

 Venus is the only planet named in honor of a female, the Roman goddess of love.

Morning Star, Evening Star

Ancient **astronomers** believed Venus was not one object but two. One was seen in the morning. Another was seen at night. Now we know Venus is the brightest planet in our sky. This is in part because the clouds in its thick atmosphere reflect sunlight. Venus is also bright to us because it is the planet closest to Earth. Only the sun and moon are brighter than Venus.

Venus shines alongside the moon in the skies near Buenos Aires, Argentina.

Earth (left) and Venus (right) are nearly the same size, but the planets look very different. Earth's surface has liquid water, but Venus's has none.

Venus and Earth

Venus is only about 5 percent smaller than Earth. Venus's circumference, or distance around, is 23,627 miles (38,025 kilometers) at its **equator**. By comparison, Earth's circumference is 24,873 miles (40,029 km). So you can see that Earth and Venus are very close in size. They're also both **terrestrial** planets, made up largely of rock and metal. However, that's where the similarity ends.

Venus does not have the oxygen or water necessary to support life as we know it.

Venus is the second planet from the sun. Earth is its neighbor, the third planet from the sun. The planets appear similar because of their atmosphere and size. However, Earth is the perfect place to support life. Venus is just the opposite. Nothing can survive in its hostile environment. Venus also has no moon. In fact, it is one of only two planets in the solar system without a moon. The other planet is Mercury.

From Venus to the Sun

Venus's **orbit** is slightly **elliptical**. As a result, the planet's distance from the sun changes. At its closest, Venus is about 66.8 million miles (107.5 million km) from the sun. At its farthest, Venus is 67.7 million miles (109 million km) away. Venus is about 30 percent closer to the sun than Earth is. Therefore its year, or the time it takes to complete one orbit around the sun, is shorter than Earth's year. One Venusian year is only about 225 Earth days.

Although Venus's orbit is elliptical, it is more circular than Earth's is.

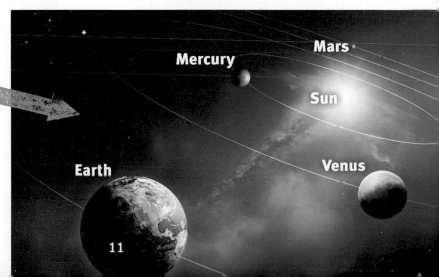

The four planets that orbit closest to the sun, including Venus and Earth, are terrestrial planets.

Mercury

Mars

Sun

Earth

Venus

A Day on Venus

Venus rotates clockwise on its **axis**. This means that it rotates from east to west. As a result, the sun rises in the west on Venus. Most planets rotate counterclockwise. So on Earth and these other planets, the sun rises in the east. Only one other planet in our solar system spins clockwise: Uranus.

Venus rotates clockwise, but orbits the sun in the same direction as Earth.

Venus

Earth

Venus spins in the opposite direction as most planets, including Earth.

The sun takes a long time to rise on Venus.

Venus's rotation is very slow compared to Earth's. In fact, Venus spins once on its axis for every 243 times Earth spins. This slow rotation makes a day on Venus very long. A day is the average time between one noontime and the next noontime. On Venus, one day lasts 117 Earth days. This means Venus experiences two sunrises in about one Venusian year.

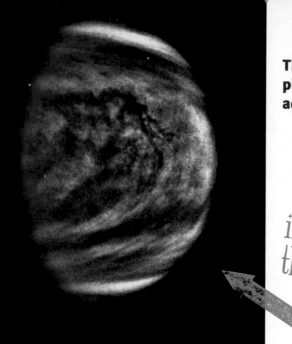

The *Galileo* spacecraft took this picture of Venus. Blue color was added to highlight cloud formations.

Spacecraft photographing Venus need special instruments to see beneath the planet's cloud layer.

Heavy Atmosphere

Venus has a thick atmosphere. Air pressure on the planet's surface is 90 to 100 times greater than on Earth. Standing on Venus would feel like being under 0.5 miles (0.8 km) of water. The pressure would crush you. The atmosphere includes deep layers of clouds. The main cloud layer can extend more than 40 miles (64 km) above the planet's surface. An upper cloudy haze can reach another 10 miles (16 km) into space.

Seasons

The seasonal difference on Venus is almost nonexistent. Seasons are the result of a planet's tilt on its axis. Earth's axis is tilted at 23.5 degrees. Each **hemisphere** receives more direct sunlight than the other at different times of the year. Venus's axis tilts at only 3 degrees. So sunlight warms both hemispheres almost equally. Heat trapped in the atmosphere keeps the temperature hot across the entire planet all year.

Venus's axis is almost straight up and down as it orbits the sun.

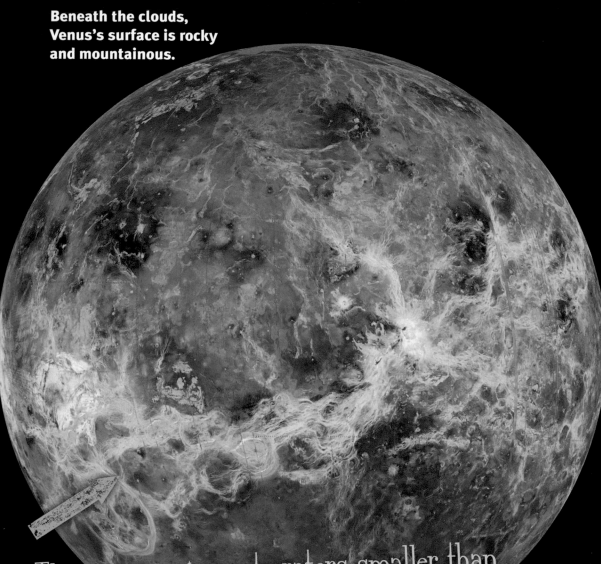

Beneath the clouds,
Venus's surface is rocky
and mountainous.

There are no impact craters smaller than 1.2 miles (1.9 km) wide on Venus. Small meteors burn up in the atmosphere before reaching the surface.

CHAPTER 2

A Hostile Environment

Venus is named for the Roman goddess of love. But nothing on the planet's surface is loving. Its atmosphere is mostly carbon dioxide. Humans and animals need oxygen to breathe. On Earth, plants absorb carbon dioxide and give off oxygen. But no plants grow on Venus. It is too hot, the clouds block the sun, and there is no water. With no plants, the carbon dioxide is not turned into oxygen. So the atmosphere remains toxic to human life.

Why So Hot?

The temperature on Venus is so hot it can melt metals. In fact, it is hotter than the planet Mercury, even though Mercury is 31 million miles (50 million km) closer to the sun. Why does this happen? Mercury has barely any atmosphere. There is nothing to hold in the sun's heat after the sun sets. So Mercury's surface temperatures range from −279 to 801 degrees Fahrenheit (−173 to 427 degrees Celsius). Venus is just the opposite.

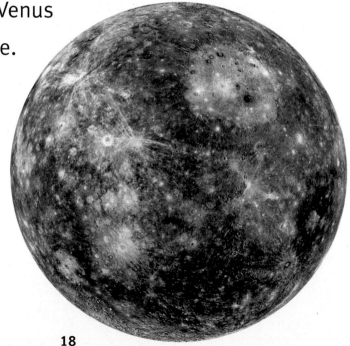

Mercury is covered in craters because it has no atmosphere to protect it from objects crashing into it.

Carbon dioxide in Venus's thick atmosphere reflects heat back to the planet's surface, keeping surface temperatures high.

Venus's atmosphere is 96 percent carbon dioxide, 3 percent nitrogen, and 1 percent other gases. It wraps around the planet like a blanket. Heat from the sun passes through and becomes trapped. The planet cannot cool down at night. This process is called the greenhouse effect. As a result, the surface temperature on Venus averages 865°F (463°C).

Some volcanoes on Earth release sulfur dioxide, which is turned into small amounts of sulfuric acid in our atmosphere.

Dangerous Clouds

When scientists first spotted clouds on Venus, they believed the clouds were water vapor like those on Earth. Data from space **probes** proved otherwise. The clouds, floating as low as 20 miles (32 km) above the planet's surface, are made of sulfuric acid. This acid is poisonous to humans. It corrodes, or eats away, metals. It also causes the atmosphere's yellow appearance. These deadly clouds cover 100 percent of the planet's surface.

Hurricane-force winds can reach 224 miles per hour (360 kph) in the upper atmosphere. These winds push upper clouds rapidly around Venus. Clouds on the planet generate violent lightning storms. Space probes launched by the European Space Agency (ESA) have detected flashes of light. They have also confirmed electrical activity. Occasionally, sulfuric acid rain falls. It evaporates long before it reaches the planet's surface.

Wind speeds barely reach 6 mph (10 kph) near Venus's surface.

Lightning travels among clouds and to the surface on Venus.

Seeing the Surface

Space probes use radar and other techniques to see through the planet's cloud layer and map the surface. The data reveals more than 1,500 volcanoes. Some are more than 12 miles (19 km) wide. They were once highly active and may have supplied the planet's sulfuric acid. The entire surface has been shaped over millions of years by volcanic flows.

There are around 1,000 craters on Venus. Lava flows may be smoothing the surface.

Spacecraft have found old lava flows on Venus that stretch for miles from the volcano Maat Mons.

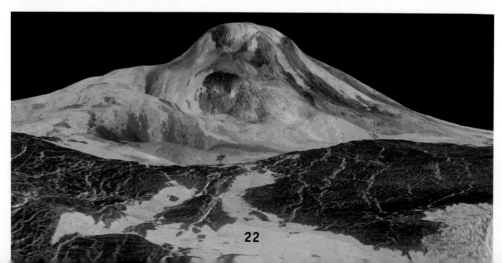

This map of Venus is colored according to the height of the land. Vast plains appear in blue. Higher land is yellow and red. Ishtar Terra appears in the upper right of the image. Aphrodite Terra is in the lower left.

Venus has two elevated areas similar to Earth's continents. One is named Ishtar Terra. It is in Venus's north and is the size of Australia. Aphrodite Terra is the size of Africa and is at Venus's equator. Combined, both areas cover only 8 percent of the planet's surface. The rest is rolling plains and lowlands. These areas may look similar to Earth. However, Venus's intense heat and toxic atmosphere make the landscape far from friendly.

Maxwell Montes is located on Ishtar Terra.

High and Low

Venus has several mountain ranges. The largest is Maxwell Montes. It is 540 miles (869 km) wide and 7 miles (11 km) high. That is more than 1 mile (1.6 km) higher than Mount Everest in Asia. Deep channels cut across Venus's valleys. Some may have been formed by lava flows. They often resemble rivers on Earth. The longest is the length of South America's Amazon River. But unlike the Amazon, the channel is empty and barren.

Spacecraft have spotted depressions in raised surface features. These hollow areas are called pancake domes. They were formed by underground lava. Venus is also covered with coronae and craters. Coronae are round or oblong areas of land surrounded by trenches. They are found only on Venus and on a moon orbiting the planet Uranus. Venus's craters were made when large meteoroids crashed to the surface.

The *Magellan* spacecraft took this photo of pancake domes dotting Venus's surface.

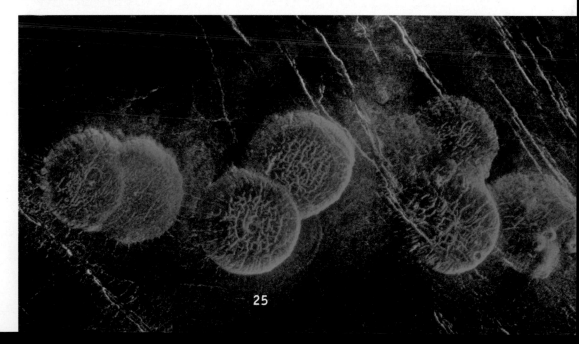

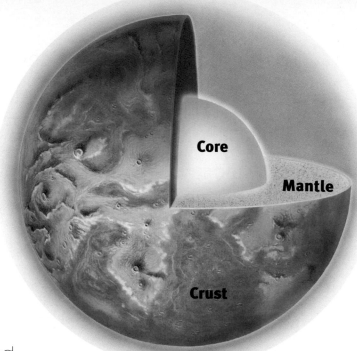

This illustration shows Venus's basic layers.

Core

Mantle

Crust

Inner Layers

Venus has three basic parts: crust, mantle, and core. The crust is the thin outermost layer. Below it is the rock mantle. Below that is the core. Scientists are not sure whether Venus's core is liquid or solid. Venus's magnetic field is extremely weak. Earth's much stronger field is created by **convection** in the planet's liquid outer core. Venus's weak field may be due to a completely liquid or solid core with little or no convection.

The Greenhouse Effect

Think of a car in the summer. If it sits in the sun all day, the interior feels hotter than the air outside. That is because the car traps the sun's heat. An atmosphere works much the same way. Some heat is required to support life on Earth. However, too much can lead to major climate changes. Certain gases, such as carbon dioxide, trap more heat than others. Temperatures and carbon dioxide levels are increasing on Earth. Venus's carbon dioxide atmosphere may hold clues to Earth's possible future.

Greenhouses are used to trap the sun's heat in cold climates.

Volcanic Venus

We know from lava flows that Venus's volcanoes have been active in the past. How active are Venus's volcanoes today? Scientists have found evidence of eruptions as recent as the 21st century. How did the scientists do it? They measured sulfur dioxide levels in Venus's atmosphere.

Most of Venus's sulfur dioxide is in its lower atmosphere, where little sunlight reaches. But in the late 2000s, scientists noticed a sudden spike in sulfur dioxide levels in the planet's upper atmosphere. What sent it so high? The source may have been one or more very recent volcanic eruptions.

On Earth, volcanic eruptions release sulfur dioxide gas into our atmosphere. The gas does not last long there. Sunlight quickly changes this gas to sulfuric acid.

CHAPTER 3

Watching Venus

Ancient astronomers knew of five planets. The one we know today as Venus seemed to follow the sun. The Sumerians thought it was related to the queen of the heavens, Inanna. They called it "the radiant star on the horizon." The Babylonians named it after Ishtar, daughter of the moon god. Some European astronomers believed it was two stars, an evening star and a morning star. The Greeks named them Phosphoros and Hesperos.

 The goddess Ishtar was associated with rain and thunderstorms.

Mysterious Object

The Mayans named this "star" after Kukulcan, the saint of warfare. They built pyramids to observe its movement. Their sightings led to a calendar that is accurate to within hours of our current calendar. The Greeks realized the star was one object, not two. They named it Aphrodite. This was the name of their most beautiful goddess, the goddess of love. The Romans called the planet Venus, after their goddess of love.

The Mayans built temples to the planet Venus.

Galileo discovered four moons of Jupiter and many stars using a telescope he built himself.

In 1610, Italian astronomer Galileo Galilei realized Venus was not a star. He was experimenting with a newly invented spyglass, or telescope. Looking through it, he noticed that Venus had phases similar to those of Earth's moon. At the time, most people believed Earth was the center of the universe. But an earlier astronomer, Nicolaus Copernicus of Poland, thought all planets orbited the sun. This idea was unpopular. Galileo's observations of Venus helped prove Copernicus's theory correct.

We can sometimes see Venus as a black dot traveling across the sun. This is called the transit of Venus. In 1761, Harvard University professor John Winthrop traveled to Canada to see a transit not visible from Massachusetts, where Harvard is located. In 1769, another transit of Venus was visible in Massachusetts. Harvard's telescopes had been destroyed in a fire. But scientist and politician Benjamin Franklin located a new one while visiting England, allowing Winthrop to study the 1769 transit.

Rare Transits of Venus

When Venus passes in front of the sun, the event is called the transit of Venus. It occurs when Venus travels directly between the sun and Earth. Transits of Venus take place in pairs spaced eight years apart. There is more than a century between each pair of transits. The most recent transits occurred in 2004 and 2012. The next one will happen in 2117. Why are transits of Venus important to us? They provided the first accurate measurements of Earth's distance from the sun.

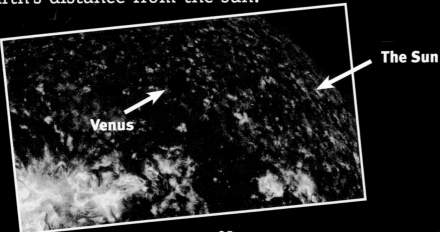

Venus

The Sun

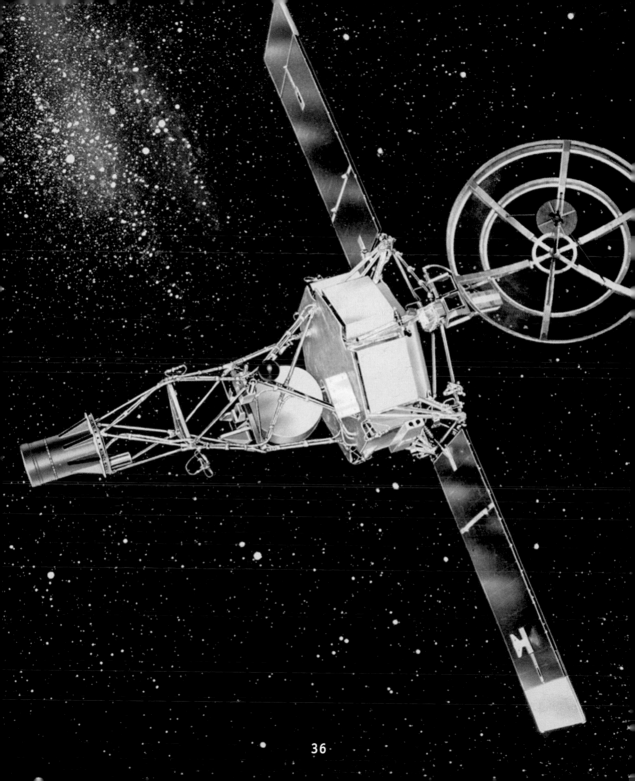

CHAPTER 4

Visiting Earth's Neighbor

Venus is our closest planetary neighbor. However, it was not until the 1960s that technology was advanced enough to allow a closer look. In fact, scientists still thought the planet was Earth's twin until we sent probes. The National Aeronautics and Space Administration (NASA) launched *Mariner 2* in August 1962. On December 14, the spacecraft passed Venus on its way to Mars. It was the first probe to gather data from a planet.

Mariner 2 was sent into space after *Mariner 1* failed shortly after launch.

Making a Landing

While the United States studied Venus from above, the Soviet Union tried landing on its surface. In 1961, the Soviet Union launched the first of 16 *Venera* space probes. Contact was lost with the first three. In 1967, *Venera 4* entered Venus's atmosphere. It released thermometers, barometers, gas gauges, and radio transmitters. It was destroyed 15 miles (24 km) above the planet's surface. *Venera 5* and *6* met with similar problems.

Timeline of Modern Venus Exploration

1962
NASA launches its first space probe toward Venus.

1970
Venera 7 launches the first object to ever land on a planet.

In 1970, *Venera 7* released a capsule to Venus's surface. The capsule recorded data about atmospheric pressure and temperature. It was crushed 23 minutes later. *Venera 8* sent more data in 1975 but was destroyed in 50 minutes. That same year, *Venera 9* finally took the first photographs of the surface. In 1983, the Soviets launched the twin orbiting spacecraft *Venera 15* and *16*. These orbiters mapped the planet's northern hemisphere.

1990–1994
Magellan maps 98 percent of Venus's surface.

2006
Venus Express goes into orbit around Venus.

2010
Venus Climate Orbiter is launched.

More Visitors

In the years that followed, Russians, Europeans, and Americans sent many probes to Venus. It is one of the most visited planets in our solar system. The missions included *Galileo*. This spacecraft was launched from the space shuttle *Atlantis*. It took a survey of Venus on its way to Jupiter in 1990. The *Magellan* spacecraft mapped 98 percent of the planet's surface from 1990 to 1994.

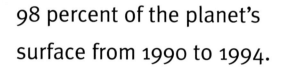

Magellan was built using spare parts from Galileo, Viking, Voyager, and other spacecraft.

The shuttle *Atlantis* is launched from Florida, carrying *Magellan* inside.

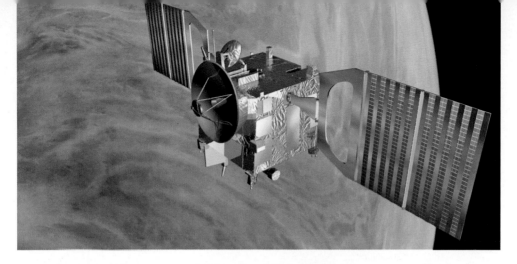

It took *Venus Express* 155 days to reach Venus.

Ongoing Missions

In 2006, ESA launched its first probe. *Venus Express* was designed to take a closer look at Venus's atmosphere. It studies the atmosphere's relationship to the planet's surface and to outer space. Soon after it began collecting data, scientists combined **infrared** images from *Venus Express* with maps created by *Magellan*. The data suggests that Venus may still have volcanic activity. Scientists hope to apply *Venus Express*'s data to our understanding of climate change on Earth.

Akatsuki **is launched from southwestern Japan.**

Akatsuki means "dawn" in Japanese.

In 2010, Japan Aerospace Exploration Agency scientists launched the orbiter *Akatsuki*. The spacecraft is also called *Venus Climate Orbiter*. Its purpose is to analyze the planet's meteorology, or weather patterns. The orbiter missed its target in December of that year and went into a temporary orbit around the sun. Its next chance to enter orbit around Venus is in 2015 or 2016.

Learning how other planets in our solar system have formed and changed over time helps us learn about our own planet. Venus may have started out just like Earth. Now greenhouse gases make it impossible for life to exist there. Scientists worry that human activity on Earth will create similar problems. The more we know about Venus, the better prepared we could be to save our own planet! ★

Studying the greenhouse effect on Venus can help us predict and lessen similar environmental changes on Earth.

True Statistics

Location of the highest elevation on Venus: Maxwell Montes, at 35,400 ft. (10,790 m)

Location of the lowest elevation on Venus: Diana Chasma trenches, at –1.6 mi. (–2.6 km)

Width of the largest crater on Venus: 168 mi. (270 km), the Crater Mead

Highest recorded temperature on Venus: 880°F (471°C)

Highest recorded wind speed on Venus: 224 mph (360 kph)

First successful Venus probe: *Mariner 2* in 1962

First successful landing on Venus and transmission from the surface: *Venera 7* in 1970

Total Venus missions attempted as of 2013: 44 (20 successful, 24 failures)

Did you find the truth?

T The sun rises in the west on Venus.

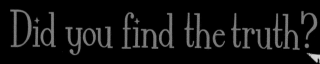

F The magnetic field on Venus is the same as on Earth.

Resources

Books

Aguilar, David A. *13 Planets: The Latest View of the Solar System*.
  Washington, DC: National Geographic, 2011.

Arlon, Penelope. *Planets*. New York: Scholastic Reference, 2012.

Visit this Scholastic Web site for more information on Venus:
★ www.factsfornow.scholastic.com
Enter the keyword **Venus**

Important Words

astronomers (uh-STRAH-nuh-muhrz) — scientists who study stars, planets, and space

atmosphere (AT-muhs-feer) — the mixture of gases that surrounds a planet

axis (AK-sis) — an imaginary line through the middle of an object, around which that object spins

convection (kuhn-VEK-shuhn) — the circulation of heat through liquids and gases

elliptical (i-LIP-tih-kuhl) — in a flat oval shape

equator (i-KWAY-tur) — an imaginary line around the middle of a planet or other body that is an equal distance from the north and south poles

hemisphere (HEM-i-sfeer) — one half of a round object, especially a planet

infrared (in-fruh-RED) — a type of light energy that is outside the visible spectrum at its red end

orbit (OR-bit) — a path an object travels around something, especially a planet or the sun

planet (PLAN-it) — a large body orbiting a star

probes (PROHBZ) — tools or devices used to explore or examine something

terrestrial (tuh-RES-tree-uhl) — relating to land as distinct from air or water

Index

Page numbers in **bold** indicate illustrations

About the Author

Christine Taylor-Butler is the author of more than 65 books for children including the True Book series on American History/ Government, Health and the Human Body, and Science Experiments. A graduate of the Massachusetts Institute of Technology, Taylor-Butler holds degrees in both civil engineering and art and design. She lives in Kansas City, Missouri.